Education Centered
Community Focused
Project Driven

a nonprofit education collaborative

A CLL & PCSB Partnership Anthology
The Plankton Energy Web: Teachers Learn and Write
Authors: Mary Osborne, Kathleen Rankin, Alicia Abelow, Bobbi Harrison, Katie Davies, Marcia Caldwell, Michele Wanger, Theresa Russo, Donna Blanton, Joseph Rober, Roseann Sacino, Timothy Slaughter

Developmental Editor: Trace Taylor
Plankton Energy Web Curriculum Writers: Trace Taylor, Mary Osborne, and Kathleen Rankin
Instructors: Trace Taylor, Mary Osborne, and Kathleen Rankin
Project Manager: Mary Osborne
Managing Editor: Trace Taylor
Production Assistant: Susan Gilbert
Design and Layout: Tysha Lewis
Technical Proofreader: Lind Archipov

Images: Cover Image: Shutterstock, FreeVectorStock.com, Carl Chun

ISBN 13: 978-1537691411
ISBN 10: 1537691414

First Edition, September 2016

Education Centered
Community Focused
Project Driven

COMMUNITY
LEVERAGED LEARNING

a nonprofit education collaborative

Innovative, Project-Driven

Workshops

*Focused Thematic
Writing Experience
Tailored to Fit Your
Curriculum*

Sentence Construction
Paragraph Construction
Essay Construction
Self-Editing
Point of View
Syntax
Vocabulary
Voice and Tone
Punctuation
Grammar
Tense
Research and Citing
Character Development
Scene Development
Active vs. Passive
Emergent Writing
Position Paper
Personal Narrative
Research Paper
Book Writing

*Full Publishing
Services to
Meet All Project
Needs*

Professional Instruction
Mentorship/Coaching
Developmental Editing
Proofreading
Layout and Design
Illustration
ePub Creation
Photography
Digitizing
Project Management
Copyright Filing
Rights Management

*Workshops result in
published thematic
compilations of
participants' works.*

Special Thanks
to:

Mary Osborne

Trace Taylor

Lisa Yacso

Paula Bellin

Kathleen Rankin

Special Thanks
to:

Smokin' J's BBQ

SMOKIN' J'S
BBQ
REAL TEXAS BARBEQUE
5145 Gulfport Blvd., Gulfport, Florida 33707
Tel: 727-329-8624

Ask About Sponsorship

Trace Taylor

AMERICAN
READING COMPANY

Sponsor an Author or Workshop

MetLife
Foundation

Ask About Sponsorship

727-367-3702

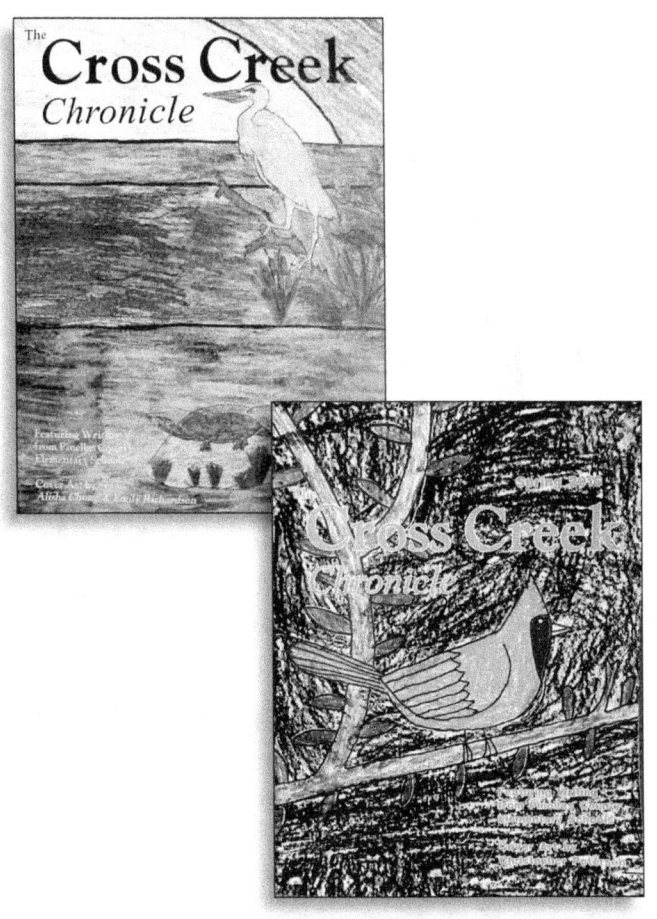

The Cross Creek Chronicle is a literary journal sponsored by Pinellas County for Pinellas County students. Cross Creek's Managing Editor, Mary Osborne, serves as a Staff Developer for PCSB and as a board member of Community Leveraged Learning.

FOREWORD
BY
MARY OSBORNE
INSTRUCTIONAL STAFF DEVELOPER, ELEMENTARY EDUCATION, PCSB

This book is unlike any other. For one thing, it doesn't have one author; instead it has eleven plus one invisible writer. That invisible writer is Trace Taylor, and before I can clue you in on what you're about to experience when you open the first pages of this book, I feel compelled to introduce you to Trace.

Trace is that rare combination of enthusiasm, vision, and true talent. She is passionate about reading and writing, and it shows when she stands in front of students to talk about these practices. Her passion for teaching and helping young people is obvious. I first met Trace when she invited me to be a judge for a competition she was offering to student writers. The winning writers would have their work bound and published in a real book. But Trace went beyond just holding a simple writing contest, she also offered free workshops every Saturday for more than two months leading up to the deadline date. She wanted to make sure every interested student, no matter their writing ability, had an equal chance. Trace truly cares about helping children fall in love with writing. This book proves she has that same desire for teachers.

On a Friday in June, 2016, more than two dozen fourth and fifth grade Pinellas County teachers gathered at Eckerd College to spend seven hours in a training titled, Project Based Writing and Publishing. They'd been instructed to bring their favorite writing tools: paper and pencil, iPad, or laptop, it didn't matter. They spent the morning learning about food webs from Trace who had created a power point worthy of an award from the National Science Teachers Association. She walked teachers through each colorful and fact-filled slide. However, walked is too pedestrian of a word to describe Trace's presentation style. She belted out the facts with fervor, "A food web is an organism overlapping an organism overlapping an organism ad infinitum." We knew we were in for some fun.

So although the morning was spent immersed in the language of food webs, this training was really about the language of writing —about having teachers write themselves. Food webs were the vehicle to help teachers get their pencils scribbling or their fingers tapping out words across a page. Once those words took up a page and then two and then for some three, the real purpose for the day began. However, many of these teachers didn't realize this was what they'd signed up for. One teacher motioned me over. She whispered that she felt very uncomfortable. Writing had never been easy for her, she said. I wanted to put my arms around her and reassure her that writing isn't easy for anyone. But, I promised her nothing bad was going to happen to her if she just tried.

We were all writing first drafts and first drafts are just that, a first try. With a bit of reluctance, she promised to stay. And although she was hesitant, she stuck it out. That takes a lot of courage. I'm proud to say her final piece is part of this book. Each piece of writing herein reflects some level of courage. And like the children Trace has nurtured through the publication of their words, these teachers now have their work bound and published as well.

For most, if not all, I imagine this book may be the first time any of these teachers have ever seen their words in a professionally published form. This book is written by teachers for teachers to use with their students. It has the potential to become a teaching text in fourth and fifth grade classrooms around the country where students are studying food webs, the plankton energy web to be more specific. But it also has the potential to teach much more. This book has the ability to prove to teachers everywhere what writer Katie Wood Ray says in her book, *The Writing Workshop: Working Through the Hard Parts (And They're All Hard Parts)*, "What is so much more important than that we be great writers is that our students see us as people who think writing is a worthwhile thing to do, as people who believe in the effort it takes to write things that really matter." What greater gift could teachers give to their students? And so, it is my pleasure to present this book to teachers, students, and to all readers with great pride.

—— Mary Osborne

I am a literacy instructional staff developer for Pinellas County Schools where I have been a teacher for the last 38 years. As a staff developer, I conduct teacher trainings, in-school side-by-side demonstrations and literacy coaching sessions with teachers. In addition, I help develop the elementary reading and writing curriculum for our district. Each year I publish *The Cross Creek Chronicle*, a literary magazine that publishes selected writings from elementary students and teachers in Pinellas County.

Education:
M.A., Elementary Education, University of South Florida, St. Petersburg, Florida 1995
B.S, Early Childhood Education, Wheelock College, Boston, MA, 1975

Workshops, Committees, Consultation Work, and Presentations:
- Board Member, Editor, Curriculum Coordinator at Community Leveraged Learning, 2012-Present.
- Presenter at Poynter Language Arts Institute, July 2014-2016.
- Accepted and Participated in UCF Coaching Institute, Orlando, Florida, August 2013.
- Instructional Materials Adoption Committee for Language Arts, January 2013.
- Writing Rangefinder Committee Review Team Member, Florida DOE, May 2012
- Editing Committee Member for the K-5

Civics Modules for Language Arts & Reading, October 2011.
- Writing Workshop presentation, Shorecrest Preparatory, St. Petersburg, Florida, January 2010.
- Writing Workshop presentation, Brooksville, Florida, June 2009.
- Presenter for Title I Parent Involvement Conference, Tampa, FL, November 2008.
- Accepted to Participate in Teachers College, Columbia, NYC Coaching Institute for Writing, May 2007.
- Presenter for Teachers College Reading and Writing Project Saturday Reunion, April 2005.
- FCAT Writing Committee Review Team Member, Florida DOE, April 2004.
- Curriculum Correlation work, Maupin House Publishers, April 2003.
- Consulting and Curriculum Development, St. Petersburg College, Tarpon Springs Campus, 2003.
- Writing Workshop presentation, Croton-Harmon, New York Schools, March 2001.
- Consulting and Teacher Training, Hot Springs, South Dakota, November 2000.
- State Instructional Materials Adoption Committee for Language Arts, June-November 2000.
- Writing Workshop presentation, International Reading Association, May 1998.
- Writing Workshop presentation, Florida Council of Teachers of English, October 1997.

- Writing Workshop presentation, Florida Reading Association, October 1996.
- Writing Workshop presentation, International Reading Association, April 1996.
- Writing Workshop presentation, Florida Reading Association, October 1995.
- Writing Workshop presentation, Duval County Schools, January 1995.
- Writing Workshop presentation, National Council of Teachers of English, November 1994.
- Writing with Voice presentation, Florida Reading Association, October 1994.
- Writing in Response to Reading presentation, Florida Reading Association, October 1993.

Publications:
"Living a Literacy of Thoughtfulness." Statement: The Journal of the Colorado Language Arts Society. Volume 35, No.3, (Summer 1999): 3-5.

"Reflection as an Agent for Change." Florida ASCD Journal. Volume XII, (Fall 1993): 42-46.

The Keys to Good Writing. Connecticut: Really Good Stuff, Inc., 2011.

Writing On Purpose. Connecticut: Really Good Stuff, Inc., 2012.

Mangroves: Teachers Learning and Writing, 2015, CLL Press, Community Leveraged Learning. 2015.

The Plankton Energy Web
2016 PCSB Teachers
Learn and Write

Food For Thought
by
Kathleen Rankin

In my large Irish family with 7 siblings, the dinner table was a survival zone, especially when my Aunt's family with 9 children joined us for Sunday brunches. Adaptation was vital if I wanted to get the grub. I loved my Mom's homemade biscuits, but they always came out of the oven at intervals, and since my arms didn't extend long enough to reach the basket, I was left imagining the warmth and flavor of her hot buttery biscuits while everyone else tasted them.

When my children were young, we took them to the Washington Zoo. My youngest son stood in awe over the gorillas being served their lunch and wondered how they would get the fruit all cut up for them in the wild. We had a discussion about the zoo keeper's role and the differences between attaining food through a food chain in a natural habitat and being fed in the zoo.

I recently went to a training this past summer with two colleagues, Mary Osborne and Trace Taylor of Community Leveraged Learning. The workshop focused on thematic writing. Our theme was the Plankton Energy Web. This professional development experience inspired me to promote creative writing integrated with science content for our struggling students.

Various pallets of delectable morsels filled with intriguing and engaging themes for our naturally curious students to bite into is the key to exploring informational texts. "Knowledge is food," stated Trace Taylor. Writing is a dynamic part of a vast system that allows our students to hone in on the craft of writing, utilizing essential thinking skills.

That Saturday morning in the workshop, we talked a lot about communities and how organisms in a community are linked through what they eat and what eats them. Some of the smallest organisms too often taken for granted and foundational to the planets energy web are plankton. A Great White Shark wouldn't exist without plankton, and neither would we.

The fundamental source of energy is the Sun. Light is food. A food chain is a single pathway that connects producer with different levels of consumers. All life on Earth is connected to the ocean and all of its inhabitants in this way are connected to the sun.

A typical marine food chain is as follows: dinoflagellates convert energy from the sun by photosynthesis into food. The Copepods feed on the dinoflagellates and transfer the energy to Sunfish when they eat the Copepods. Small sharks feed on the Sunfish. In turn, larger sharks feed on the smaller sharks.

The biotic levels of an ecosystem are: producers, consumers, and decomposers. Feeding relationships are often identified as simple food chains. These relationships are actually more complex. Food webs are the links between the producers, consumers, and decomposers.

The more that teachers can encourage students to value the little things, educate them on the vast and vital ocean and teach them how their lives are woven into this feeding relationship of an ecosystem, the more power we have to feed the next generation. Now isn't that some food for thought!

Giant Jelly Bloom
by
Alicia Abelow

I used to explore a clear, cool, blue sea, but now I float through garbage drifts. A combination of kelp, oil, plastics and other garbage create a new ecosystem. Home was never a maze of waste and litter until the humans decided to use it as a garbage dump. Humans come to take pictures with me on their exotic Japanese vacations. Come Dive with the Giant Jelly. Since humans have been coming into my world, it no longer looks like the utopia it once was. What are these dangers that enter my perfect world?

My 450-pound body needs to be nourished to support my size. My habitat used to be a paradise of plankton, larvae, fish, and other jellies, but now my food supply declines as my numbers of brothers and sisters grow, and humans strip the sea of life. I hope the food will always be here for us to eat. While hunting, I have to be careful though in case a hungry leatherback sea turtle spots me and decides I'm dinner.

In the summer months, I travel with others in groups called blooms. As the blooms grow in number, we come in conflict with the humans, especially in the cold seas around Japan and China. We prefer the cold arctic waters and rarely venture into the warmer gulf streams, but I'll need to adapt to survive.

Tiny, Yet Mighty
by
Bobbi Harrison

There are two types of plankton in the world, phytoplankton (micro plants) and zooplankton (tiny animals and animal larvae). Krill falls into the zooplankton category. Many people think of krill as a lowly, nameless, faceless creature, at the bottom of the food web. Yet, krill is one of the most important pieces of the Global Food/Energy Web, part of a large community of arthropod subphylum, Crustacea. These small, shrimp-like crustaceans fuel the engine of the Earth's marine ecosystems. As of today, there are about 80 species of krill known to exist. Without krill, most other sea life would cease to exist. Krill swim in swarms, primarily as a defense mechanism. The surface of the ocean can turn pink and red from their vast numbers. Krill can live up to 10 years, an amazing longevity for such a tiny creature. They spend part of their lives avoiding predators in the cold depths of the ocean, some 320 feet (100 meters) down while the rest of their time is spent on the surface with the phytoplankton.

Female krill lay up to 10,000 eggs at a time, sometimes several times a season. Krill larvae go through four stages of development. After hatching, larvae rely on yolk reserves for their nutritional needs during their first two stages, the nauplius and the metanauplius. The krill are made up of 3 tagmatas, or parts: the cephalon or head, the pereion or thorax, and the pleon or abdomen. The body has a chitinous exoskeleton, a calcium carbonate shell some describe as translucent. Their large compound eyes are important for finding food, but also for avoiding ferocious predators. They have two antennae, gills, and several pairs of thoracic legs called pereiopods or thoracopods that appear in the third larval stage, or calyptopis stage. Five of these legs are used to swim while the others are used to feed. Furcilia is the final larval stage. During this stage, the shrimplike krill develop into adults. When fully grown, their miniature figure and colossal eyes can fit on the tip of a human finger. Being no bigger than 2 inches long is a real benefit when escaping from a blue whale or a fish.

Like many other zooplankton, krill feed on phytoplankton (micro plants), thereby using the primary production energy that the phytoplankton derives from the sun. Don't get all grossed out, but whale poop, that's right, whale poop, is another major food base for krill. Whales eat up to four tons of food a day. Imagine the size of a baleen whale and how much poop they get rid of a day. That's a lot of food, Yum, Yum! In order to obtain their food, krill gather it and use a filter feeding method. They filter their food from the water using their front legs. These legs act like combs, which allow them to separate out the edibles.

Krill is a mainstay food resource for whales, seals, penguins, squids, sea birds and fish. Even humans eat krill. They taste salty and a bit stronger than shrimp. In Japan, krill is called "okiam" and served on rice. People in the Philippines ground the krill up into a paste called, "alamang". Krill oil is another product, packed full of essential omega-3 fatty acids, which can be found in markets. However, recent studies show that krill populations decline at a rate of 1% each year. Disturbances in our ecosystem play a big part, such as increased water temperatures due to climate change and the decline of whale populations. The extinction of whales would mean the extinction of one of the most integral parts of the food web. So let's keep the Global Food/Energy Web strong by protecting the whales. Protecting the whales means plenty of food for the krill.

Vampire Squid

by

Katie Davies

Carl Chun, 1903

I am older than the dinosaurs who once roamed this planet. "Eat, survive, move, eat, survive, move," this mantra runs through my brain. I dwell in the gloom of the deep pelagic zone, murky depths force colossal pressure upon my body. Food is life and mandatory for the continuation of the species.

Others hide from me. I sense their presence as they sense mine. Measured movements, I am furtive in my travel, which occurs when others in the oxygen minimum zone are still. We vampire squid dwell in the earth's ocean depths and are the last of our order. My official name is vampyromorphida, but vampire squid is my common name. Formal name vampyroteuthis infernalis, mollusca is my phylum, oxygen minimum zones, my domain.

Some may look down at us for our harvest of decayed flesh, fecaes and detritus known as marine snow. The lower edge of the Global Food Web takes place in this sunless, poorly oxygenated place. I consume tasty bits that drift down to my world and settle upon my sensory filaments. Some may think of the vampire squid as a poor example of the Global Food Web, but we know the role we play. Someone must pick up the little pieces.

My body expands, moves and flows. I float with my cape suspended, allowing my spiny tentacles to stretch and expand. My webbed tentacles make my survival possible. I am able to wrap my legs up over my head like a cape and present my sharp underspines to any predator who thinks it might want to eat me.

My body has been unchanged for three hundred million years. Its structure gives me the ability to absorb the pressure of the deep. The bio luminescent discharges give me a few seconds to escape from and my legs are able to regenerate if one gets lost in an attack.

I am a marine snow eater. Live prey holds no appeal, but I appeal to others who hunger near me in the dark depths. I sense someone coming closer, so I move away quickly, but not quick enough. I am always the prey. My contribution to the Global Food Web is my energy and that energy flows without end.

WHALE POOP FOR DINNER
BY
MARCIA CALDWELL

Not many animals eat whales, but many animals eat whale poop. Whales play a significant role in our planet's food web. When a whale poops, it releases an abundance of nitrogen and iron chelate into the oceans. Phytoplankton, which inhabits the photic zone, and zooplankton, which primarily feeds in this same zone, need these minerals to survive.

Left over faeces becomes marine snow. Marine snow drifts to the bottom of the oceans where it is absorbed by marine life in the benthic zone. Marine snow is an important source of energy for many benthic dwelling species such as crustaceans and gastropods.

The number of whales corresponds to the quantity of plankton in the ocean. Many animals both on land and in the oceans are dependent on plankton as their food source. Less plankton means less food, and less food for plankton means less food for all the planet's animals, including humans.

Seabirds swoop down into the ocean for fish that have eaten nutrient packed whale poop then they fly inland over a nearby farm of strawberries or potatoes where they drop their poop. The soil is enriched by the iron and nitrogen in the bird poo. The strawberry or potato plant absorbs these nutrients from the soil, and I get to eat a delicious, nutritious strawberry. The vital nutrients in whale poop travel from the oceans to the land through animals, and this fertilizes our planet and provides me with healthy foods.

Sometimes, the birds accidently drop pieces

of their fish in a field of grass. The soil absorbs these nutritious bits, and then the grass absorbs them from the soil. Then a farmer puts his cows in the field, and they eat the grass. The farmer then takes the nutritious cow milk or cheese or meat to the market where I buy it and take it home for dinner.

Tonight I'll have mashed potatoes and steak and maybe strawberry shortcake for dessert. Less food for plankton means less food for everyone. The disappearance of whales reaches further than we can imagine. From ocean to table, whale poop influences life on Earth.

CREATIVE CRITTERS
BY
MICHELE WANGER

Humanity could not survive without tools. Implements like hammers, screwdrivers and Allen wrenches help people achieve their goals. Tools make it possible to build, work, and play. For example, the swing set in the backyard provides hours of fun for our family, but without wrenches, a hammer and a battery-operated drill, assembly would be next to impossible. Some people believe that humans are the only species to use tools, and others believe that using tools requires fingers or at least hands. Research is proving that both of these beliefs are inaccurate.

It's tough to crack open an oyster or clam or the hard exoskeleton of a big crab. Otters use rocks to hammer them open. Like other members of the weasel family, otters have strong paws to take advantage of tools such as driftwood and broken pieces of glass bottles. These are all tools otters use to get at the meat they most prefer to eat. Otter pups learn tool use from their mothers.

Some dolphins are known to use tools. Some of these cetaceans search coral and shell reefs for food. They also like to sift through the sediment for hidden fish and stingrays. To prevent injury to their sensitive snouts while they search, they wrap sea sponges around their noses for protection from scrapes and cuts by urchins, coral, and rocks and from the danger of stingray tails. That's pretty innovative! These dolphins are called spongers and differ from many other dolphins because their diets are completely different from non-spongers.

Tool use demonstrates dexterity, creativity,

problem solving skills, and intelligence, qualities we once believed only the human animal possessed, but new research proves that we still have a lot to learn.

Sea Turtle Journey
by
Theresa Russo

Salty air swayed on the breeze and caressed the skin of a young girl on the beach at Little Gasparilla Island. Untouched by the effects of commercial high-rises and tourist pollutions, this paradise welcomed her for a second summer in a row. Her family gathered on the beach of gray sand, admired the view of the Gulf of Mexico, and planned their activities for the week. They had arrived at their favorite place on Florida's west coast.

Two days into their summer vacation, island locals approached the Saint Petersburg family. Afterwards, the family learned these local heroes consisted of 10 to 15 members called the "Turtle Patrol Team". Two of these members happened to live adjacent to the family's rental home. That night, after sunset, the crew planned to release a group of loggerhead hatchlings back into the Gulf of Mexico. The family accepted an invitation to witness the miraculous event.

Later that night, everyone met on the beach. The patrol team asked the eager little girl to hold the flashlight and point it at the water. The hatchlings scuttled towards the glimmering light. The girl realized that she had helped the baby loggerheads reach the safety of the surf. Later that night, after the little girl put on her pajamas and climbed into bed, her mother told her about the loggerheads and the marvelous sea in which they live.

"The loggerhead turtles gathered together for safety and warmth and prepared for their entry into the sea. Adventure awaited them. Human hands held them gently and positioned them on the sand near the shore. One by one they waded into sea. The first turtle entered into the dark abyss and felt frightened. The second plummeted into the water with a clumsy curve. The third and fourth stayed close to each other and dove down deep.

The turtles searched the sea for algae-like sea mats called Sargassum, crucial to their survival. Sure enough, they found it and grew into strong Loggerheads, each at least 250 pounds! They learned to eat crustaceans such as blue crabs and gastropods such as snails, scallops, clams, and oysters, some even learned to eat sea urchins. Learning to eat new things helped the turtles survive."

The mother softened her voice to a low whisper and revealed the following: "My dear child, we must handle this ecosystem with care. We must remember the delicate balance of life on Earth. These turtles are precious, and so are all living organisms. The survival of the turtles depends on the smallest plants and animals in the marine ecosystem, the plankton. Humans must realize we all have a purpose in the delicate balance of life, no matter how small. If we destroy one organism, we destroy many organisms."

The girl woke up early the next morning with purpose and dashed towards the water. She searched wildly for the turtles she released the night before, but the rise and fall of the waves were all that greeted her. She thought about what her mother told her the night before and felt adoration for a world she could not see. A seed of inspiration grew in her heart and her mother's words echoed in her mind. She walked towards an old can on the beach, picked it up, and carried it to the trash can.

Vampire of the Deep
by
Donna Blanton

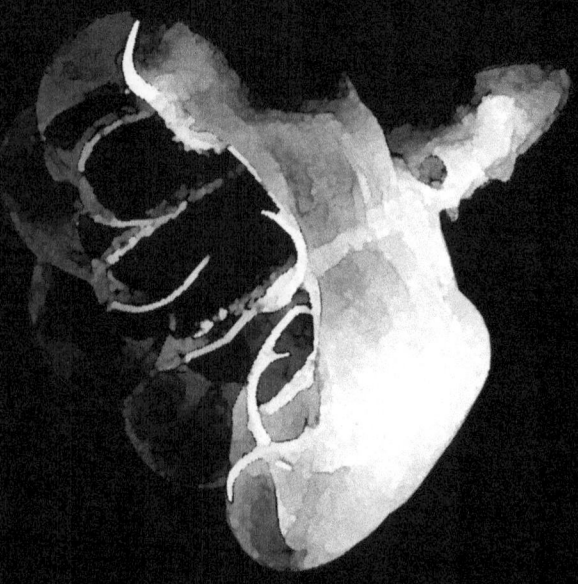

Artist Unknown

"Tell another one! Tell another one!" The squid campers chanted over and over again.

Buddy loved all of the attention he received at the Squids summer night campouts. He loved to tell scary stories about the deep dark seas.

"Okay, okay, I have another story for you," he announced.

A hush fell over the group.

"This one is really scary," he warned. "It was a day just like any other day. Schools of fish circled us. We looked for food and safe places to hang out."

"There's nothing scary about that," they all shouted.

"Let him tell the story," one squid yelled.

Buddy blew some bubbles and continued, "All of a sudden my cousin, Wendy, zipped by in a panic."

Everyone's eyes widened.

I took off after her. "What's going on?" I asked.

In a steady voice, Wendy replied, "I saw one."

"At first, I imagined a whale, maybe a gigantic squid, but when I saw how bad she trembled, I knew exactly what she saw, the creature that dwells in the deepest part of the sea, down deep where the sunlight fades into the darkest dark."

"Wendy saw a..." word-by-word Buddy whispered, "vampire squid. They are not a squid like us but they are in our family line along with octopuses."

The little squids squirmed, "Vampire squid? There's no such thing as a vampire squid, is there?"

Buddy swirled as he rose to gain attention and gulped some water. "No such thing. Oh, they're down there, alright, way down deep and you better be careful, too. The vampire squid comes at you at speeds of 12 inches per second. You can't see them coming. Their jet black or reddish purple bodies help them hide in the dark water. You swim for your life if you see one, and when you think you're safe, presto! Right in front of you, all lit up, flickering on and off like Christmas lights, a vampire squid."

None of the baby squids moved.

Buddy drifted to the center of the group and spun around with each dramatic sentence, "When they catch up to you, their giant blue eyes sum you up and down." Buddy swam close to the group and opened his eyes real big while he spoke.

The group gasped some water in fright.

Buddy swam around the circle. "Just as soon as you think the vampire is ready to attack you, they let out a glowing cloud of mucus from the tips of their arms and disappear."

Mouths gaped open in horror.

Buddy closed in for the finale, and pointed over everyone's head and shouted, "Look out! There's a vampire squid behind you!"

They all screamed, "AHHHHH!" and dashed behind Buddy, but laughed when they saw it was just a jellyfish going by.

"That was scary!"

The group settled back down, and the youngest squid asked what they all wanted to know. "So, do vampire squids really exist?"

Buddy looked at everyone's faces, "You'll just have to swim down into the deep, deep dark and find out for yourself."

~~~Swish~~~

No Trophies for the Hunter

by

Joseph Rober

On a cold winter morning, an elephant seal mother waddles into the sea with her calf. She has the wisdom of experience. She knows the danger and her scars tell the stories of past escapes, old fights for life. The sea churns with peril, but she must go forward. The calf must learn to swim, to hunt. The crowd of elephant seals gives shield and in they plunge. The calf lurches and follows her in rolling loops. They bask for a minute until the ocean quakes. The seals scatter away from the gray shadow that appears from the deep with many rows of sharp teeth. A bloody meal for the shark means a sad, painful return to the herd for the mother.

For six days straight, an albatross flies from England to the tiny Island of Kerguelen, just north of Australia. From the sulfuric smell in the air from Lake Rotorua, he knows he is almost there. The albatross rests atop the rolling water unaware of the rises from the depths to meet him. A wave cracks open and rows of teeth swallow him with a cruch and snap.

A baby sea turtle faces the threat of birds, raccoons, opossums and dogs before it ever reaches the sea, or maybe it will be led away from the sea by false moonlight and die in the dunes from starvation and dehydration and be eaten by rats. A few babies make it to the water where the ocean offers the possibility of life, and then one day, while the turtle nibbles on a jellyfish or a coral, along comes a tiger shark and the turtle's life is over.

The great white shark swims mostly

unchallenged. Well-fed and unafraid, it goes where it wants unbothered except by the ocassional fisherman. An orca mother with her baby appears. The great white moves in for the kill, but out of nowhere comes a third bigger orca that slams into the shark's left side. A fourth appears and slams the shark from above while the mother leads the baby to sa safe distance. It's three against one. He tries to flee, but more orca join in and take turns hammering the great white until it's dead and becomes food for other life in the sea.

Anita the Arthropod
by
Roseann Sacino

Most people get their food from a store. This is a fortunate luxury for humans. My thinking was the same until I met Anita. Anita might be just another girl with a human name. However, she is an arthropod, a stone crab to be exact. Arthropods are invertebrate animals that have an exoskeleton, a segmented body, and jointed appendages (legs). Arthropods include insects, arachnids, myriapods, and crustaceans.

Anita lives in the Gulf of Mexico, and like me, she is native to the Florida coastline. When I first encountered her, she told me the story of her existence and explained how all life began in our splendid oceans. I was volunteering on a beach cleanup. I poked my hand into a rock crevice for a piece of trash.

Anita screamed, "Ouch!"

A talking crab! I was shocked at first but soon told her about the cleanup project. She proceeded to tell me her life story. She obviously had a lot to get off her barnacled exoskeleton.

Like all crustaceans, Anita did not start off with a strong exoskeleton. Her muscles and armor became secure when she reached her juvenile stage. She started off microscopic and endured many dangerous adventures just to survive. My Mom and Dad nurtured and cared for me, but Anita didn't have parents to care for her like I did. She spent her childhood, her larval stage, as meroplankton in the plankton drift. This means that Anita was not destined to stay small. Meroplankton are subdivided into benthic, those that settle on the bottom; demersal, those that swim near or above the bottom; and pelagic, the open ocean swimmers.

In her larval stage, she drifted with the currents in the photic region of the water column where sunlight and phytoplankton nourished her growth. The fate of her brothers and sisters were less fortunate. They were swallowed by whales, dolphins, and sharks in gulps of water or caught and eaten by jellyfish. Sharks are generally considered to be meat eaters, but I learned first hand from Anita, many fish and mammals eat all sorts of phytoplankton and zooplankton.

Anita, now an adolescent, left the plankton drift and chose the rocks of the jetty to hide in. Stone crabs, like Anita, are in demand by many animal species including humans. A fearsome event occurred when an octopus crawled up onto the jetty and grabbed one of her claws with its powerful tentacles. Luckily a large wave washed up and allowed Anita to pinch herself free from the cephalopod's grasp. I admit, when I first saw Anita, I pictured a cup of warm butter and a set of crackers, but Anita made me realize that the lives of all the animals in the vast ocean are part of a global food web, and all life serves its purpose in that web. I understood and now, thanks to Anita, respect the incredible connection between all organisms in the Gulf of Mexico.

Anita's story enticed me to learn about other organisms that live in the ocean with her, and I have begun a personal journey to learn more about all the animals who share the planet with me and play a role in the global food web.

The Adventures of Aqua Girl
and Splash

41